A BROKEN WOMAN "SHE IS NOT"

A Broken Woman
"She is Not"

*Take it or leave it,
it's Your Choice!
But, It's My Story,
My Truth!*

YOLANDA C. AVERY

YoSugga Sweets Production, LLC

Contents

Thank you, God, for allowing me to share my
light with others!

My dearest companion, confidant, and partner in
life, this message is for you. Your generosity has
touched my heart and I will forever be grateful for
everything you have given me. I am immensely
grateful to you for taking the time to guide me
and for sharing your valuable insights that have
opened up a whole new world of possibilities for
me. Thank you. Embracing my skin and accepting
who I am has enabled me to become a stronger
woman, and your support in that journey has
been instrumental.

I truly appreciate the fact that you have given
me the freedom to express myself not only
within our family, but also in the entire world.
Throughout our growth as individuals and as a
couple, your love remained unwavering. Despite
walking this journey alone, my inner strength
and resilience keep me from feeling lonely. You
were subservient to God's work. I am committed
to serving his word. Your spiritual guidance and
God's love will be my companions as.

I continue my journey. I am the one who must travel this path. With the knowledge and gifts you have given me, I embrace it all. I walked through everything with God's Will as my guide and protection, and his love as my comfort. I will always speak the truth while healing with love and light.

I am sending you a rose straight from my heart, my love!

C. Avery

Introduction

Have you ever looked up the definition of what a broken woman is? I have, and there are several speculations on the internet about what defines a broken woman. I read somewhere that a broken woman is someone who takes vulnerability to an uncomfortable level. It seems like she needs to be taken care of because of her damaged behavior. Another one said that a broken woman has depleted her heart, mind, and spirit.

Well, if that's the definition of a broken woman, I guess you can say I am broken. I never thought that your heart, mind, and spirit could become depleted; Or shall I say exhausted? I like that word better. Because that is how I feel when situations defeat me or I cannot control them, and I have used up all my energy. True enough, I have been through heartache, sorrow, betrayal, and confusion; Yet I am still here, standing. Now, if that's the definition of a broken woman, I know plenty of broken women. I can remember being accused of being a broken woman by a broken man and he did not even know it. Because men have a way of concealing their pain. Society has led some men to believe that it is a sign of weakness to show feelings. But that's another subject for another time or another book.

I reached a point in my life where I had asked myself if I was broken? I had to step back and really look at what I was doing wrong in my life. I give love where love is given. I help others that need help. I show compassion for my peers and those who cross my path. So, is it wrong for me to want to feel those same feelings in return? Is that the reason I am being accused of being a broken woman? Because I voice for respect and stand for what is right? I believe all women deserve respect. Some of us have to work hard to demand it, especially us black women. Being a black woman, they often misjudge us as being difficult, too independent, or too demanding. Now, I will not sit here and defend all the reasons these allegations are untrue, because the fact is that some are true. I know for me it is true. And why not? Don't I deserve the right to not settle for just anything? If it was not for women who were built with this caliber, many people would not be in productive, positive, and stable relationships today. True enough, those are not the main foundations of a relationship, but they are important assets to the relationship.

Now, I will admit I have had some issues growing up in my life. Some things I had to overcome, but who hasn't? Alot of those issues defined who I am today and who God wants me to be. I will open up and tell you about some of those issues that put me on this path and how God uses people and situations to know his plan and nothing else. So, if you think this book is about me criticizing those who have wronged me on my journey, close this book immediately. Because that is not what this is about.

This book is about some past issues of my life's journey that I had to push through or, some would say, get over it. This is the story of a woman who faced obstacles alone and found her purpose in life.. It also gives a glimpse of my connection with my spiritual guidance.

I will say it now and probably say it again for those in the back. I am not here to criticize or bash anyone negatively in this book. I will speak on my truth in my story. I will speak about the energy I received. So that means if our encounter altered my spiritual journey, rather it be positive or negative, it's in this book. Take it how you want, but it's my truth, my story. I am only doing what God has ordered me to do. Touch a life, heal a heart, or inspire a journey. This is my purpose. I would do as thou will. Someone may be going through a similar situation and I am here to show that God's love never wavers nor leaves you. I will say it again: I am not here to criticize or bash anyone negative in this book.

Chapter One

First Encounter

Let's go way back to when I was young. I would say probably my primary years. The years when everything was new to an adolescent mind. Seeing the world and people with innocent eyes. Playing hopscotch in the street and not having to look over your shoulders worrying about strangers coming to take you from your "used to". Young enough to know when something was not right, but not young enough to understand the magnitude of deception and violation through a child's eyes.

It was a time when life was good. Growing up in two-parent households, thinking that was the norm because everyone on our street had both parents in their household. Majority of the parents had jobs. The children on our street were like family. We could go to each other's house and play for hours. Our parents never had to wonder or worry about us because they knew the neighbors. They were our extended family. You know the ones; they can call your parents when you are doing wrong and they have the authority to whoop you just like your parents.

During that time, there was no such thing as children's rights. Or, I'm gonna call the cops. Even if you were bold enough and mentally challenged in the head and you called the cops, that's a whole other situation you created for yourself. Nine times out of 10, the cops may know your parents. They will come and handle it themselves. Or, they may tell your parents and stay to watch the main event that is about to happen where your behind is the star. The cops would stay and watch this long, drawn-out ass whooping that is taking place right in front of them. They did not blink an eye. The kidding part is you think the police are there to serve and protect your ass. Nah, they are waiting on that cold beer your dad promised them when he was done whipping your butt. They would then sit back and have that cold beer on your porch with your dad, laughing at how he almost passed out whooping your ass. And to top it off, you would be the joke of the neighborhood for the next 72 hours. Because by then someone else would have done something stupid too. And no, it didn't happen to me. My dad didn't whoop girls, but I saw it happen to someone else.

Let me get back to my story. I loved playing outside. It was fun playing in the dirt just to be free. I could play with my brother and his friends, as if I was one of the boys. Yes, I was a tomboy on most days and others I had to be a girl for recitals and ballet practice. Even back then, I knew I was different. Now I know you are probably thinking "different? How is she different?" I was not a follower but a leader, doing things my way, and not sticking with the norm. I always had unexplainable things happen to me growing up, and even so, to this day.

My first experience was the firecracker incident. This is a true story. I was playing with my brother and his friend in the backyard one day. We had some leftover fireworks from the previous holiday. It was my brother, his friend (Randy), and me (the lookout). I am always the lookout. They decided they were going to pop the skyrockets out of their hands to see whose rocket could go the furthest. My job was to watch and let them know who was coming. So, being who I am, I wanted in on this fun. I complained to them and told them if I could not play; I was going to tell it on them. Come on now, don't act like you don't know the code of being the little sister or brother: "I am telling if you don't let me play." So, of course, they gave in. They handed me a smoke bomb. That's the most boring thing to do. It only puts out colorful smoke, and that's it. My brother was like, "You said you wanted to play." I could not argue with him. He was right. I just wanted to be part of the fun. So, he gave me the bomb and told me to hold it in my hand while he lights it up with a match. If you ever lit up a smoke bomb, it puts out a powerful spark. That spark hit my middle finger. I let out a loud scream and threw that damn thing to the ground. In my moment of screaming, smoke came out of my nose and mouth. Randy was pointing at me saying, "look at your sister, she weird." They were looking at me, with this wtf just happened while they were cracking up with laughter. I had a weird feeling, but something was comforting me. I could see something angelic in the surrounding smoke. It was like a presence of protection was there. I got a blister mark on my finger that day. I never cared about popping fireworks again. I learned later that was my first encounter with the Divine. Later in life, they would show up again.

Chapter Two

Trauma Within

Going to grandma's house was always special for me. That's where your first love is created, if you are blessed to know your grandparents. I know some would say parents. There is no argument there, but that love is automatically given during the birth of your creation. I am talking about as a person being able to tap into a connection with other people that is merely created by actions of love, trust, and guidance. Grandparents' love is just built differently. This is where you are treated with unconditional love. They spoil you. They listen to you without judgment. Not to mention they will give you anything you want. It's a sanctuary place for a grandchild. I can remember my mom telling me the story of how she had to go claim me back from my grandparent's house. She purposely kept me from them. My grandfather came to my mom and dad's house and asked my mom if I could visit my grandmother because she was heartbroken without me.. Of course, she gave in. I am glad she did. For that, I have several beautiful moments with her. That was my beginning and the foundation of experiencing unconditional love.

My mom and dad both had full-time jobs and because of that, it involved baby-sitters. I would go to my mom's parents' house and my brother, who is a few years older than me, he would go to my father's parents' house. This is where we would spend our time when our parents would be working. I loved being at my grandparents' house on my mom's side of the family. This was a house of adventures. We always did something new every day. She made sure that I had my favorite snacks at her house, too. What better way to bribe your grandkids? Grandma would dress me up and we would go places. I remember some does it will be in the country with other family members. Sometimes, we go fishing.

Over time, life circumstances changed significantly. That period of my life ended came to a close when my grandmother passed away, leaving me with a profound sense of loss. I found myself under the care of my aunts, my mother's younger sisters, following my grandmother's departure. While my parents were occupied with work, they stepped in and took care of me diligently. Although it was challenging, it became clear that a change had to be made, as they also had their own lives to live. I really didn't want to make this change, but unfortunately, it was necessary. Yes, even young children have feelings and hate change. My aunt's role they played in my life was that of filling a void that my grandmother had left vacant. My parents were working they could not do it. Don't look at this in a bad way, because it wasn't. My parents had worked hard to provide us with the best of everything, and for that, I am truly grateful. Homelessness and hunger have never been a part of our lives, as we have been lucky enough to always have a place to live and food to eat. It was me that was the problem. I was different. I had the foundation of experiencing unconditional love and protection from family members that I clearly thought were my parents.

Since I practically lived at my grandparents' house for so long, I thought that was home for me. So, when that major change had entered my life, it was devastating. It was my "use too." And my true home with parents was like being with foster parents. For me, it was the beginning and ending of a new life for me. So now it's time for other family members to pitch in for our well-being. Which was okay with me. I loved being around family.

But this one particular day change my life. Change me. Little did I know that this would affect me in my adult years. It was the first time that I ever saw my dad get out of character. For me, it was a day that my favorite cousin and I would never play anymore because of no fault of hers. It was a day that changed my personality and changed who I might have been or what I could have done with my life. All because my grown ass cousins took my innocence away. A day I could never stop smelling that fetid, musky smell, nor the pain it caused me mentally and physically. Something I carried for years. Okay, I am just going to say it. Family members molested me and I did not really know what it was called back then.

This is how I remember that day. My dad's side of his parents' house was the go-to destination for my many cousins and me during our summer vacations, and those memories have stayed with me. Grandma's house was a safe and loving place for us while our parents worked. At least for the moment, I thought. My grandma, on my father's side, and aunt were in the kitchen baking cakes, my favorite pastime at grandma's. On this day, my favorite cousin was not there that day, neither were her siblings who I also liked to play with. When they were around, they always looked out for me. Rather, it was being afraid of the giant dogs in the neighborhood or the pesky little boy next door.

Now, I've only told this story to a few people in my life. I guess you can say I was afraid to talk about it. I wanted to just throw it under a rug and never think about it again. Let's just say it never left me. It was something that I had to work through in order to understand what was going on with me and affecting relationships in my adult life. We will talk about that later.

I remember walking with my older cousins to another aunt's house. I can't remember why we were walking to the house. But it was something they did often. See, one of my aunts stayed down the street. When we got to the house, they told me to change my clothes because I was dirty. Which was true, I had been playing outdoors all day, and I was filthy. So, I did what I was told to do because they were older and they knew better than me. After I got out my clothes, they told me to lay my naked body down on the table so they can dress me. They did things to me that should not have been done. I will not go into the details of it, but I can tell you even though it's been over forty something years ago, I can still remember it as if it happened yesterday. There is a blockage that I cannot remember anything afterwards other than telling my parents. I can remember telling my mom and dad what they did to me that day, and it wasn't right.

That's when the phone calls started. I remember talking to a stranger every day on the phone. For the longest, I thought it was an uncle of mine. I never recall seeing him. I just remember getting a phone call every day from a man, asking me about my day. He was always nice to me and listened to what I had to say about my day. I could not understand why my parents did not have an issue with me talking to this stranger on the phone. They never questioned it. So, I assumed it was a family member I had never seen before. Why a family member? Because he asked me about members of my family and knew them by their names. It wasn't until later on in my life that I realized the individual I had met was a therapist. I did not realize that until this year, when my husband mentioned it to me. I had talked about this incident a few times with my husband. My husband helped guide me through this traumatic situation. Yes, forty something years later, it still held me hostage. All this time, it never dawned on me that the man was a therapist.

I hated that ever happened to me. No child should never have to experience anything like that. It could affect you all of your life. I never went back over to my grandma's house again until I was much older. I remember my mom telling me a few years later how upset my father was the day that it happened. He had grabbed his shotgun to deal with them in his own way. But my mom talked him out of it. Now I clearly understand why I have memories of having tea parties with my father. It was his way, I assume, of trying to put the childhood of innocence back into me. It worked for the moment, but those moments would creep back up later in my life.

Chapter Three

Become A Woman

It wasn't until later in life that I came to the realization that the devastation I experienced during my childhood not only impacted me but also had an effect on the people who took care of me. Unfortunately, I was unable to go out and spend time with my friends. Only a few selected ones. My life became very restricted. For that, I became furious with my mother. I thought she was showing favoritism to my siblings instead of me because I can do nothing. I hated her for it. Whereas, they had time to enjoy life and go with their friends; Me? I just stayed in my room, listened to music, and read books. It didn't dawn on me until later in life that the reason my mom was so restrictive on me was because she was protecting me; protecting me from the world, and protecting me from anything that could've done me harm. Back then, I couldn't see it. I clearly see it now that I am an adult. During that period, I was recognized solely as the rebellious child who always went against the norm. I was just different in my thinking. Observing the entire experience from the front to the back, from ins and outs, and from side to side. Analytical thinking is what it is called today. That is how I process information. It's the part of me that wants to know the "why." I am very thankful to my mom, to this day, for being so strict with me. It taught me how I can be by myself and not lose myself in my own thoughts. When Covid hit a few years ago, many people could not do that. So many people have committed suicide because they did not know how to be in a place of solitude to themselves. Society has created a social life for people needing other people's energy to sustain their way of living. They hold the belief that they cannot manage things on their own and must seek help from others. I am definitely not that type of person. I master the art of solitude. COVID has proved over and over that it was not for the weak.

The restricted lifestyle of growing up had its negative aspects, though. Not being familiar with, as they say, the street life. Book sense, common sense, and street sense are three types of knowledge. While I had the first two, the last one was missing. So, with that situation, came the not knowing the ways of people. That everyone is not like you. Some people have that sense of running games and doing whatever means of getting what they want. That knowledge could have possibly helped me when I went to college. I was naïve, which allowed me to fall prey and be a victim, once again, letting the life of the unknown take me from the mission at hand. Which was getting a college education.

So here I am going to college; Working at a fast-food joint, when not in class, and having a boyfriend was my life. I didn't stay on campus because I was told it was better and cheaper to be at home. Besides, my mom clarified she was not signing any student loans for me because she had done that with my brother and he never finished school. She would not be responsible for any more student loans. So, I had to do it for myself. I worked and whatever I could not pay for myself; I used Pell Grants to help pay for the rest. To this day, I thank you, Mom, that I did not have to worry about those pesky student loans back in the day. Dodged that bullet!

Okay, back to the story. Since I was handling my own school affairs, I was still naïve about the world of dating and a lot of things I still did not know. I was not experienced or educated about relationships and sex. Let's just say my first time having sex of my own will made me become a woman. Yes, I was pregnant.

After that, here comes the talk, or shall I say the gossip? The discussions people were having about my life. One thing about me, I never concerned myself with what others say about me. I was used to it. If people really knew me, they would know I am not a gossiper. We can talk about anything you want, and I won't gossip about your affairs. I'll only disclose information about you to rectify a misperception about you or a situation involving you. I would hope someone shows me the same courtesy. The talk among my siblings was that I got pregnant on purpose. Of course, they did not say it directly to me, but that was their discussion when I was not around. Yeah, your own family can talk about you too. It was my sister that told me about this discussion years later. I had to inform her I never got pregnant on purpose.

Sex was never a discussion in our household. The only thing you heard constantly was not to get pregnant. No one ever sat down and explained the ins and outs of procreation. It was not something that you can go look up on the internet because that was not available back then. Hell, I got my period on the first day of school going into junior high. That day, I thought I was dying. My mom gave me this pad to put in my underwear and to make sure I change it throughout the day. She told me this was normal, for every girl that turned my age was going to get one. If I ever did not have one, there is going to be a problem with me and her. That was just great. Another thing I had to worry about with her. So, for someone who made it all the way through high school and graduated without having a baby was a milestone for me. It was not until I was a few months away from becoming a freshman in college that my aunt took me to the doctor to get birth control. After that visit, I remember getting a packet of pills to take every day and never missed a day of taking them. Just remember, still no one ever told me about sex and I never asked. I was not told that you have to be on these pills for quite some time to work. I knew nothing about a condom. How did it work? I was shelter. But my first husband was open and willing to educate me. Thus my firstborn.

This story is for young girls who get caught in having to be something they are not ready to become. Don't let anyone or peer pressure order your steps. Know that your life doesn't end because of the choices you make. So, what if you are not wanting to do something? Keep yourself pure if that is your choice because, at the end of the day, you only have to answer to yourself. Don't let other options in life steer you away from your chosen path. Accept and enjoy the journey that's ahead of you. It's not a catastrophe. You gotta accept it and become the woman that God's gonna help you become. Lots of women have been through this, and there are tons of stories we don't know. You're not alone. People have been in your shoes before. Just do what we all do: choose your shoes, walk in your girl magic, and make your history, journey, story, and truth!

Chapter Four

You Heard
that Too

Man, this right here woke me. Spirits are always working, no matter the day or the hour. When I was a single mom, I always tried to make family time fun with my kids. Every Friday, my children and I chilled out. Sometimes we would find ourselves in the country at my ex-husband's mother's house for the weekend.

Oh! I forgot to mention about my first marriage. Nope! I didn't. Just nothing to talk about on that subject. Other than that, sometimes mistakes can bring out beautiful experiences (the birth of my children and an angelic mother-in-law).

Back to the story. After working long hours of work during the week. I would always try to make Friday nights special with my children. That was our time. I let them choose what we eat, the movies we watch, and the games we would play. I did not want them to focus on the downfall of being in a single-parent household. I wanted to create good and fun memories as a family so they can do the same for their children when they become parents. After a fun-filled evening, it was time to get some sleep. We had a busy day ahead of us.

After having a good night with my children. It was time to get the next day started. Saturday mornings always involved house cleaning, washing clothes, going to the grocery store, and taking care of other errands. But before I get out of bed, I always look over the day before and give thanks for the blessings I received on that day. I always thought about what I can do better on this day than the day before. It was something I had learned years ago from a pastor at church and watching my father's mother pray every day of her life.

Not to get off the subject, but this is how some of us in my era learned about God's obedience by watching those grandparents. I witnessed my grandmother, as old as she was, getting on her hands and knees and kneeling by her bed every morning to pray to God. I remember asking her why she prayed to him in the morning and not at night like we do. She told me she prays to him at night as well. The reason she prayed in the morning was because she was giving him the glory of letting her wake up to be of service to her family. That knowledge remained with me forever. So that is one reason I always pray to do better than the day before.

Back to the story. So, as I am lying in bed, I hear a voice, a man's voice. It said really loud, "Get up!" That scared the shit out of me. I opened my eyes, trying not to show the panicking state I was in. Remember, I am a single mom, so there is no man in my house; just myself and my young boys. I open my eyes without moving the rest of my body, trying to remain calm and plotting out my fight skills. My oldest son on the hand raised his head and said, "Mom, you said something?" Well, hell, I guess they about to take us all out. So, I jumped up out of bed, not knowing if someone else was there in the room with us. I looked over at him and I asked if he heard it, too. He said, "Yes ma', it was a man's voice said to get up". By that time, I already proved there was no one in the house but us. So, I looked around the room, trying to pinpoint where my other two boys were. See, they all three had camped out in my bed. I was at the foot of the bed and the three of them slept at the head of the bed. As I was looking, my youngest son was not in bed. That's when the fear kicked in. We all started looking throughout the house for him. Just in time, I found him. He was about to drink out the bottle of ammonia. He had gotten out of bed, gone into the kitchen, and pulled out all the cleaning supplies. He had the bottle of ammonia in his hands when I walked into the kitchen. I rushed over to take it from him before he did anything else. After that, lesson learned, add child locks to today's errand list. A sigh of relief came over me. At that moment, I cried. I cannot remember what I was crying about. I just knew several things were happening to my existence at that moment. It's been some time since the spirit has connected with me. It was so long ago that I truly had forgotten about the connection. Thankful that God had all our lives that day. Thankful the angels were there to stop it. Thankful to know God still loved me and was there watching out for all of us. This story still gives me chills when I speak about it. My oldest son still remembers it too. He can still recall the voice just as I did that day. So, if there were any doubts about the existence of angels, spirits, and God around us, it's not coming from my family. We are true believers! Oh, and on another note from that story, my youngest son, guess what line of work he is in? Janitorial! He has his own cleaning business.

Chapter Five

Dating Goes Wrong

Be careful who you let in. I was always skeptical about who I let get close to me. Or who I let in my house. But sometimes a wolf wears sheep's clothing. I remember times my grandfather would get off work at 10:30 pm and he would drive across town to bring my children donuts and bananas. He would come to my door and ring the doorbell excitedly to give his great-grandkids his treats for them. But he did not know my number one rule. I do not care who you are. My door was not opening up for anyone. For all I knew, a thief or killer could stand there with you trying to get into my house. Remember, I was a single mom with young kids. I had to draw a line somewhere. My grandfather would leave and go to my mom's house. She lived next door. He would tell her, "You know your daughter wouldn't open the door?" She would tell him, "Yep that's true, she not opening the door after a certain time at night." She also says to him, "I don't blame her either." So, he would have to leave those treats with my mom for her to give to my kids. Okay, maybe I was a little too protective.

I thought I would try to change that theory. After all, I am only in my twenties. During that period of my life, I was still relatively inexperienced and on the lookout for the right man to start a relationship with. It had been a minimum of 5 years since I had separated from my first husband. Hell, I forgot I was even married to that guy. It had been a considerable amount of time since I had seen or had a conversation with that man. Despite the circumstances, I had a great relationship with his mom. She was the first and the best mother-in-law I ever had. I mean, I only had two, but she was the best. She was a mother to me. She taught me about a blended family. She taught me so much about life from her perspective and her journey. Her background came from Mississippi. She had so much firsthand history and knowledge. She knew and was friends with Medgar Evers. Her home was right beside the ruins of *Gone With The Wind* home. She was a founding member of Delta Sigma Theta Sorority at Alcorn State University in Mississippi. She was the one who encouraged me to date two years after my husband had just left. So, I did. I had gotten into one of those on-and-off relationships with a guy. Who I ended up having two kids with. That relationship was a roller coaster, and I had had enough. I was ready to move on from him.

It took me a moment to get back to the dating scene. I was protective of not letting anyone get close to me again. So, working every day all day was my focus. I was doing great at work. I was getting promoted every 3 to 6 months. Life was good. Until one day I was headed home from work, I stopped at a nearby gas station to get gas. I met a nice guy there. He was tall and nice-looking. He offered to pump my gas for me. He did all the right things on the first impression. He had lived in the same neighborhood as me. Maybe a few streets over. We talked about the different things we had in common. So, we exchanged phone numbers. Cellphones were not popular, we had regular house phones. We had talked every day since our first meeting. He offered to come to do yard work for me. I accepted his invitation because my yard needed it. Now we are about a month into the courting stage. He wanted to take me out on a date. Still, in my protective mood, I suggested I will cook and he could come over after I put my kids to sleep. He agreed. He came over. It was great at first. We played a board game and watched a movie. Well, it was getting super late, and I needed to get some sleep because I had a busy day the next day. As I was walking him to the door, he was in front of me. I put my hand on the knob. He placed his hand on top of mine aggressively and pushed the door back. He looked me in my eyes and said you know we are not done. I will not go into

the vivid details of it. It's a moment I won't ever forget. Nor will I ever tell this horrific moment. I couldn't
wait until it was over. Luckily, my children were still
asleep. Because they were the only thing on my mind.
Even after that night, the ordeal was not over for me.
I ended up becoming pregnant. The torment of my
nightmares of that night would not leave me. I had
some soul-searching to do. I know I did not want to
have this baby, but I felt God would punish me for
doing the ultimate sin, I thought. I made up my mind.
I could not bring this life into this world because I
knew I could never give it the love it needed. I could
not remember how this child was conceived. I did the
deed. Within the next 24 hours, I was back at work
like nothing had ever happened.

I filed those pieces of my life where everything
else was of trauma experiences. As far as the guy, I
didn't see him anymore until some years later when
my brother invited me and my husband out for an
outing. We had met up at this pizza place. As we
walked in, I saw that guy in a group with my brother
and some more friends of his. I almost passed out.
My husband caught my fall. He asked if I was okay. I
told him I was and that I just lost my balance. I don't
even think the guy remembered who I was. If he did,
he played it off really well; I thought. I couldn't stay,
but I wanted to support my brother. I cling to my
husband. My husband could sense I was not myself
and he asked if I was ready to go. Yes! I was. The drive
home was quiet. When we got home, my husband

turned off the car and told me if I ever had something I needed to talk about, he was there to listen. I shook my head and told him I know. I opened the door of the vehicle, stepped out, and remained silent. The experience I went through was so traumatic that it took me a whole 10 years before I could talk about it with anyone, and the first person I shared it with was my husband. I did not tell my brother about it either, just like I did not tell anyone else.

Chapter Six

Passing My Test

God sends people to challenge you or puts you in situations to be tested. How and when they come is not known to most. My story is actually about me being lost in a new world and the Divine putting me on a path to understand my reactions to certain relationships. It does not matter if those relationships are business or personal. He is testing us. He already knows the outcome. The outcome is for us to see it for ourselves. It's a reminder to let us know he is still and would always be in control.

It took me some years as I got older for me to realize God is working with me and through me. I remember relocating to a company that I had worked at for about 10 years. The company was expanding, and they had a management position available. I thought to myself, this is my new beginning. See, I had been through so much and needed to see the world to reinvent myself. Every corner of my home reminded me of the times I had with this man. All I wanted was to be out of this misery. So, I went and pleaded my case to my boss about why I should be offered the management position. It is the perfect solution for me to start over with my life. A few days later, I was informed that I got the position. I had 30 days to get myself packed and ready to leave.

Now it's down to the wire. I have three days before boarding a plane to start a new journey. I decided I could make the most of these days by visiting my loved ones. It started with going to see my mom. The visit was sad because my mom was in the hospital for a medical reason. So, I said goodbye and went to visit my grandmother, who was also in the hospital for a different reason. I did not know that would be my last time seeing her alive. But I cherished the moments that I had with her. My next stop was my dad. Now my dad was a stay-at-home bachelor. He had played himself out with women and was a Jerry Springer fan by day and soap operas by night guy. I was visiting him and we were speaking about his mom. I asked him if he wanted to go to the hospital. He declined, of course. My dad cannot stand going to the hospital. I said my goodbyes to him.

It was my last hour before embarking on my new journey. My boss had called an emergency meeting at the office. While we were in a meeting, I received an urgent call from my brother. He had told me my grandmother had passed away. It devastated me to hear such news an hour right before I had to be at the airport. He told me to leave and not to worry, that he would look after my father. So, I did.

It was my first day on the job. I was getting settled in with my new coworker, Chris. She was there to run the sales team. At least that's what I thought. I was getting things in order in the warehouse. Upon getting inventory counted within the computer, a delivery was made. This truck driver had presented me with paperwork stating he had a shipment for me to sign. He was a very nice older black guy. He asked me if I just moved there? I politely said yes. He invited me to come to his church. I am thinking to myself, "I don't know you, man." I smiled and shook my head and said, "Sure, maybe I will come one day." Deep down, I knew I wasn't, but he did not need to know that.

It's been 11 months since I made this long-distance decision. It turned out to be a pleasant journey for me. I was feeling like myself once again. I was making new friends and making a decent living. It was not bad at all. Life was benefiting me. I talked to my mom every day. Our relationship was in a good place. She was my voice of reasoning and encouragement, which was something I needed during my homesick days. Everything was great until this day. My boss had flown into town to check on things and to inform his plans of promoting Chris as the General Manager of the store. I was livid. How in the hell was this woman going to be my boss after I trained her on most things? Then I realized she had the qualities that most Asian men like in a woman. I should have seen it coming. Once again, another sister was kicked to the curb for being black. It did not matter that I had been at the company the longest. It did not matter that I created the inventory for every item that was sold at the company. It did not matter that I was the one who secured the plasma center deal. It did not matter that I was the one who create the isolation kit (that he now makes millions of dollars from). It does not matter that I had dedicated over 10 years of my life to this company. It did not matter that I started from the bottom and worked my way up the chain of command. It did not matter that the new general manager had only been working with the company for less than a year.

I was mad as hell (forgive my language). I knew I had to do something. This would not work for me. Because I knew Chris did not earn this job. She had not put in the time nor the labor to hold this position. I was done working for this company. They had done the ultimate betrayal. Before I made any hasty decision, I had to talk to my counselor for guidance, my mom. I told her how I was sabotaged and she listened with understanding and knew that I had the right to be upset. So, the next day I went to work. The boss and Chris had set up the conference room for a brief meeting. I was ready for what they had to say. I sat down and listened to my boss explaining what my duties would be and what Chris's duties were going to be. I sat calmly without getting upset because I knew

I had my last card to play and they did not know what I was about to say or do. But as I was listening, they were trying to make me a slave there. They were going to be assigning more duties for me to do. While Chris could do nothing but get an increase in pay plus a commission on sales that were not generated by her. I had heard enough. I raised my hand and said here is my resignation. The shock that went across their face was priceless. I told them both that they could hire someone and I would train that person as long as they pay my way back home. That meant moving my items, my children, and myself back to Louisiana and they foot the bill. We agreed on those terms. The next day, my boss flew back home.

Since my last meeting with Chris, I didn't give a shit what they did. I only did what they required me to do, nothing more, nothing less. I had all kinds of evil thoughts coming into my head. I could make life really messy for them: both the new person and Chris. I chose not to. It was not in my nature, and I did not want the bad karma to come back on me.

It was my last week there. I had survived the process. I just unlocked the door to the office. As I was turning the lights on, the office phone was ringing. There were still a few minutes before the store opened and I was wondering who was calling. I answered the phone. It was Chris's husband. He greeted me, but I can tell in his voice something was not right. He told me Chris had been in an accident the day before and she would not be coming to work. I asked him if was she going to be alright. He said he did not know. See, Chris had fallen over a balcony the other night and hit her head on the concrete. The balcony was about 3 stories down and her husband had fallen with her. But she got hurt the most. Forgive my description of this, but part of her brain was on the concrete. "Wow!" is what I was thinking. Everything I had felt about the job issue had disappeared. I felt his hurt through that call. A day I will never forget. I advised him to keep me posted and I would pray for them both. I took a moment to get myself together. I had to notify the corporate office about the issue, but they were not open for another two hours. So, I had to call my boss on his cellphone to let him know. I did not want to make this call because I knew he was still upset with me for quitting, but I had a job to do. I called him, told him about the issue, and reminded him that this was my last week here and that they need to plan on filling in for Chris. I know for a moment that he had wished that he treated me fairly, but oh well, life goes on.

As the day went by and no more news about Chris, work went on as normal. So, I thought. Remember me telling you about that truck driver who wanted me to come to his church, well he made his presence known today. He had delivery three days before my departure. Now, if you have been keeping up, the first time I saw this man was my first day at work, which was 12 months back. During my official year here on the new job, I had not seen this man anymore until today. He said, "Sister, the Lord told me to tell you, you've done well." I looked at him and said, "What!" He said, "The Lord told me to tell you, you passed your test, you can go home now." That's all he said. The only thing I could say was, "Yes, sir." I could not wait to call my mom and tell her what had happened to me. She told me I have a testimony. To me, it was more than a testimony. It was confirmation that God loves me and has a plan for me. I just wish I knew what it was. The next few days, I was back at home with a new job, a new home, and a vehicle waiting for me. When Sunday morning came, chile, I was right there up-front telling my testimony to the whole church. This journey brought me even closer to my mom. My next chapter was just beginning.

Chapter Seven

Dreamed about You

Now that I was back home, things seem to go easier for me. I had a great support system. I was working full-time. My mom and I had a great relationship. I was eating much healthier. Life was glorious for me. God had shown me all the blessings he had for me. That didn't mean the test stopped coming. There was more to come.

When I got back, I was no longer working an 8 to 5. My hours were different because I was working for another company where I would go in late and get off late. So, my normal daycare that I used would not be open late when I get off. So had to find another means of babysitting. I decided I would let my ex-boyfriend's mom keep my kids. Why not? She was great with them. Ms. Cassie was her name. This woman had a heart of gold. She was a "no-nonsense" grandma, too! She didn't play with my kids. I remember visiting her one day and telling her about how my hours at work differed from what I was used to. She said don't worry about those kids and bring them over to her house. She did not mind. Since she already was watching her other grandkids, having mine there would be no different. She never asked for any money to keep them, but I gave her some, anyway. I was going to pay someone to keep them, so why not pay her? It was a splendid arrangement. I did not have to cook when I got home because she had fed them their dinner when they were with her. One day, I arrived at her house to pick them up and her daughter was there. She said that her daughter wanted to talk to me. I said, "OKAY." I was wondering what she wanted to talk to me about. In my mind, I was hoping it was not about her brother. Before I could get it out, she immediately said, "It's not about my brother, either." She said she had this dream, and it was so real. She had told her mom about it. She said it scared her so badly because it was so real. Hold up, wait a minute before we go any further. Let me tell you a short story.

After my return to Louisiana, things were finally doing good for me. I started hanging out with my sister-in-law and brother. My brother was on this basketball team for adults. They were having basketball games. I took the kids with me a few times when my brother played. My sister-in-law was in the matchmaking stage. She would always tell me about the guys that played with my brother. How I needed to come checked them out and it would impress me to see the guys he was playing with. After one of my brother's games, they introduced me to this guy. He seems nice, I thought, but I thought they all did. Not falling for that shit again so, I was standoffish. I came too far from that last ordeal. The guy was a gentleman towards me, but aren't they all? I kept my head focused. I heard the story about how he was a semi-pro athlete, but that did not impress me at all. I continued to show support for my brother by going to these games because it was a good outing for myself and my kids. But wouldn't you know the universe has a way of throwing a curb ball at you? How could I forget about the damsel in distress signal? I ended up having a car issue, so that was a clear path for this guy to step up. And boy did he! You know that moment in the movie *Waiting to Exhale* when the guy (Taye Diggs) is taking off his shirt? I had to stop and acknowledge him at that moment. Even though I had seen him shirtless many times before, this time it felt different. I had to double-look. Or it could have been because of the moment. I mean, I needed my car fixed, so I was desperate. Yeah, that must have been what it was. But somehow, someway, he had won me over. We had communicated for about three or four months before we had any serious entanglements (shout out to Jada Pinkett). He lived in another city, and I was glad because I was still getting used to my rebirth and my independent. I loved my new life, and I wasn't ready to get into something serious.

Back to the dream. Sorry for all this skipping around, but I promise this shit ties in together. The dream she had was about me and this new guy (the shirtless one) I mentioned to you earlier. Now she had never met this guy, nor did she know anything about him. But she gave a good description of him from her dream. At that moment, she had my attention. She said the dream involved us being in a car wreck. We had hit a tree, and we both died. He was driving, and I was on the passenger side. When she was telling me about that dream, her hands were shaking as if she knew it was going to happen. She said, "I would not tell you, but my Mom told me that God had given me a message to tell you and it was my duty to follow through on his will." After speaking with her, I knew and felt that there was a message that I needed to hear. So, after talking with her about that dream, something changed inside of me. I needed to distance myself from him. Which was easy because he lived in another town and things had not been feeling right. It was like he had a dark cloud over him. Something was always causing him to have problems and issues. I felt sorry for him because he was a nice person to me, but he just had so many obstacles coming at him. I remember I was moving to another house that was in a better neighborhood for my children. He was helping me with the move. Chile, you talking about being scared and nervous every time I was around him. I just knew he couldn't drive me anywhere. I always had an excuse not to be in the car with him. The moving day could not get here quick enough. So, I prepared myself for that conversation. You know the one. That says, "Hey we need to talk" and "It's not you, it's me." That conversation. We parted as friends. It was a relief. I knew that would be my last time seeing him. I can remember it like it was yesterday. A couple of years ago, my brother called to tell me he had heard that the guy, who was his friend (the shirtless one), had passed away. I asked my brother how he passed. He told me it was an accident with a car. The car had hit a tree, and he died on impact. I was speechless and scared at the same time. That could have been me. What if I never listened to that dream? What if I had looked over his flaws and stayed with that guy? My children would grow up motherless. I hung up the phone, shocked and nervous. From that moment, I never questioned how God communicates with you. If someone had a message, I would listen. If I had a job to do by God, I would do it. With no hesitation, I think about that part of my life when I have moments of questioning my purpose in this life. I know what that purpose is now. It is to tell others about him. To let others know my stories. To be a servant of messages.

Chapter Eight

Depression Alone

At that point, depression makes its presence known. Since the age of fourteen, I have consistently held a job and have never been without employment. It all started with summer programs, but as time passed, they transformed into a necessary means of survival. The moment I resigned from my job at the age of 39, I felt like I was abandoning my financial stability, my freedom, and the way I had always supported my family. I have faced many challenges in my life, but that task was among the most difficult I have experienced. If a company is experiencing failure and you have been employed there for a substantial amount of time, you are faced with the decision to either remain until the company's ultimate demise or prioritize your own personal growth and development. I decided to prioritize myself, which is something I had never done before, and put my faith in God to guide me. After coming back home, I ventured into entrepreneurship and started my own business. I am excited to say that this was only the first of many more experiences to come.

The company where I was once employed experienced a major setback when two out of its three owners passed away. The company was transferred to another company as the previous owner sold it off. With the arrival of new ownership, we can expect new beginnings and fresh starts, which you and I both understand. With every new beginning, there is also an ending that must be faced. The things that I used to devote my time to would no longer be a part of my present routine. The individuals who have been my customers will no longer be categorized as such because of this change. At that moment, I took matters into my own hands. I opened my custom print business. It started off really well. I could secure all the customers that I had from my previous job. The problem came when I was using my own funds just to sustain the daily expenses of running a business. The overhead expense outweighed the revenue coming into the business. Eventually, I sold my customer-based business to a local business and regrouped my financial situation. So, I enrolled myself in college. I pursued an associate degree in pharmacy.

By enrolling in a Pharmacy Technician program, I could potentially put myself back on track with my career goals. The amount of time invested in that process may have been significant, but it proved to be worth it. My academic achievements led me to earn an associate's degree with honors, which is a testament to my commitment to education. So here I come, workforce, back in the flow of things, I thought. I know you are wondering, "Where is the depression at?" Trust me. It's coming, just keep reading. I started working at a local pharmacy part-time. It started out great, and it was cool working with a younger generation. My experience was positive, but I encountered some issues with the hypocrites of medicine. Although the company has a good mission statement, they, unfortunately, fall short in delivering the service that aligns with it. By constantly signing consent based on their beliefs, you were unknowingly agreeing to follow the company's beliefs, which unfortunately did not prioritize good health. So, I left. I could no longer be a part of a system that spoke one language and not lived up to the service.

So once again, I am at home. This time, it was different. I constantly was putting in job applications but could not find any work. Days went by, and then months went by, and still no job. This was something I was not used to. I was used to having my own and doing what I wanted. Some days, I would stay in bed. On other days, I would just sleep the day away. Some days I put on clothes, and other days I did not. It was not until one day I was not feeling like myself anymore. I went to the family doctor. From that day, they diagnosed me with some type of depression. The doctor prescribed me two types of prescriptions. I immediately took the prescription, thinking it could help stop feeling what I was feeling. Wrong! Instead, the medicine did just the opposite. I started thinking about death a lot, "my death" to be specific. Suicide was in my thoughts every single day. Where was my family during this time? They were around, but those who know me know that I usually keep things to myself. I am a private person. I only give out to those who I am close with and those that I trust. It had gotten so bad that there were days I would cry a lot for no reason. Something was growing in me, and I could not share or talk to anyone about it. Until one day, I remembered there was something I could do. Pray.

Prayer is the best remedy for anything that you are going through. I remember being at home alone. I went into my bedroom and got on my knees and just began crying out to God, my savior, and my protector. I prayed for help, love, guidance, strength, and any and everything that my heart was craving. It was one of the most emotional prayers I have ever done in my life. I asked God to show me my purpose, to show me what he wanted me to do. After doing a very long, snotty nose, and crying prayer, I got up, went to wash my face, and got myself ready for bed.

For the next two weeks, I started having long dreams.

My dreams were vivid with color. They were like watching movies in my sleep. I could recall the characters, the colors, the scene settings, and the smells of each image that was playing in my head as I slept. God had heard my cries. My body could feel the chills that grew within me. I had this overflowing of love and excitement that had built up in me. God was healing my depression. He was removing the darkness from within. I no longer had those thoughts of dying. My thoughts were filled with words. My mind was anxious about getting what was growing inside me out into the world. God had restored and reset me on my path.

Chapter Nine

Death by Three

2015....... This year, right here, almost broke me. The first death of the year. I remember getting a phone call from my mom telling me she had something to tell me. You already know this will not be good when your mom calls and tells you she has some bad news. At that moment, you have all kinds of scenarios playing out in your head about your siblings, your children, your spouse, or even your parents. You brace yourself for a few seconds and ask what is it?

Then she tells you that one of your favorite cousins had died. Your heart pounds and tears are filling up in your eyes while the pain in your chest aches. You are wondering all kinds of questions. How could this be? They were so young. You thought they would live forever. How would a family reunion be without their laughter and beautiful smile?

It was the morning after hearing the sad news about my cousin's passing. I woke up with a feeling of writing some type of encouraging words for my family. The anxiety was kicking in really hard and getting rest was not on the menu today. Those who get those urges know what I am talking about. God was speaking to me. The spirit had given me a task to complete. This would be my first writing piece. I shall get to work. It took me 10 minutes to come up with a poem. The words were just flowing out of my mind. I was definitely being guided by the divine. After I completed the poem, I posted it on Facebook. My family members received it well, and that was the start of my writing journey. The feeling I had that day was spiritual and I could feel the excitement in me. God had answered my prayers. April was the beginning of my journey.

The second death of the year. The month of May was always pleasant. This is the month of my wedding anniversary. Yes, for those of you who do not know, I am married. This was our 8th marriage anniversary, but we had been together a lot longer than that. Since I am talking about the year 2015, that would put our relationship at 15 years. This month, I was getting back to the old me. I had a purpose. God had given me my gift of writing and I just completed writing my first script. So, life was feeling good. My anniversary was great, as usual. My husband always made sure that day was special. But it was the next day that my world was shaking again. I received a phone call from my sister telling me she had some bad news. My heart sank to the floor when she called because I knew immediately that something terrible had happened to my mother. I can hear my sister on the phone telling me Daddy B had died. At that moment, I composed myself to tend to her on the phone, but in the back of my mind, it relieved me to know it was not my mother. Do not judge me. Some of you know exactly what I am talking about. I could not help but wonder, "What are you trying to tell us, God?" We just experienced a loss a few weeks ago and now there was another one. But I knew better than to question God's plan. I immediately went to my mother's house to be with her. Now, this time, I had no words to give to provide any comfort. I had to step in and assist my mom with preparing her husband's arrangements. The elders in the family usually would step in and address the situation. But this time my mom was the elder in need of help. So, like I always do, I stepped up and took matters into my own hands. I had to wonder why God was putting me in this position once again. The first time I was a servant of peace. This time I am a servant of work. So, I no longer questioned his plan for me. I just did what God wanted me to do.

They say death comes in threes. I never liked that myth. But this year made me wonder if that was true. It had been 6 months since my mom lost her husband. Life was getting back to normal for everyone. At least, that is what we thought. It was around midday and my phone rang. It was my mom. This call from her did not start off like the usual bad news call. She asked me how my day was. It was a 2-minute conversation. Then she goes, "I got bad news to tell you." I did not think it was something bad because I felt like she would have started the conversation off with that first. She said, "Your aunt passed away today." I nearly passed out when she told me that. See this death was very shocking. There were no signs my aunt was ill. As a matter of fact, we had just had a visit with them a few days before her passing. So, this was very unexpected.

Now this death was a hurtful one because this was a very close relative. This was one of my mother's baby sisters. This aunt practically helped raise me. I have a lot of first with this lady here. She and I were more alike. She was my first child's godmother. She taught me so many things. So, you can imagine the hurt I was feeling about this death. So, after my mom had told me, I had to regroup once again and ask my mom if was she okay. Remember, my mom had just lost her husband and now her sister. She said she was okay, but she was just concerned for my uncle. See, my uncle and aunt, had been together since they were in high school. This was the love and marriage I dreamed of having. But we save that story for another time. So once again, I jumped into the servant role. I asked my mom what I needed to do. She told me nothing that she knew of. My uncle had everything under control with the help of his kids and their family. So, we sat back and waited for the schedule of her arrangements.

This time, I was serving my own as a messenger for God. After hearing about my aunt's passing over the next few days, things were unusual for me. I was having anxiety and panic attacks for no reason. My heart would start racing for no apparent reason. It was not until one night that I knew God was not finished with me yet. I remember having a dream about my oldest son. He had been in a serious accident. I woke up with a message for him. I grabbed my phone, and I immediately started texting him. The message said, "You need to slow down; you are going too fast. If you don't slow down, you can hurt yourself." I sent that message to him around 3 something in the morning on November 2, 2015. Little did I know the message was going to be of significance later.

It was a rainy day on November 7, 2015. This was the day we were laying my aunt to rest. The service was beautiful, and the family was together once again. We all gathered at the mausoleum to have gravesite rights because the ground was wet from the rain. Soon after the repast, everyone went home to prepare for church service the next day. That night before I went to bed, my son called me. See, he was away at college. He was talking about how he felt good that night and he was going to make some changes in life. He said he was getting ready to go out and hang with some friends. I told him to be careful and remember the message I gave him a few days ago. We said our good-nights and then a few hours later, my life changed. I received a call from one of my son's friends stating that my son was in a car accident and it did not look good. The person on the other line was crying uncontrollably. The phone went dead. Oh my God, I was panicking, is my son dead? I called every emergency medical responder and police station in the state of Mississippi. No one had any information about my son's accident. Then my phone rang again. It was one of my son's close friends. He informed me that the accident was bad. I had to swell my fear and ask that no parent should have to ask, "Is my son alive?" He said, "Yes." My heart felt at ease. But he said he is not in a good condition. He told me they were getting ready to airlift him and fly him to another state. "I had to get to my son" was the only thing on my mind. Once again, God used me as a messenger servant.

After the whole rehab part of his journey, we finally sat down and talked about that night. He had told me right before his car hit the tree, my aunt, who had just passed away, showed up in his car on the passenger side and told him to slow down. They said my son was not supposed to have survived that night and when I saw the photos; they were right. Throughout the entire ordeal, I connected with strangers that day and I still have a connection with them. God will use any situation to get our attention. You better wake up and know that he is God.

Chapter Ten

Gift from God

This is the day that the Lord has made for me. It was one morning I woke up with a sudden urgency of needing to tell someone about my dream. I can remember how excited I was telling my spouse about it. I can see the characters clearly as day. I am seeing the setup vividly; the colors are bright. I can remember the beginning and the end of this dream. It was as if I was right in the middle of it, watching it all unfold. The dream seemed so real. I thought to myself, "I better write all this down." As I was writing it down, I realized that this was a good story to share, and I wished I could turn it into a movie. "Why not?" I thought to myself, "Other people do it." How can it be?

This dream happened right after the poem I did sometime in April, right after hearing the passing of one of my favorite cousins. I gathered a notebook, a couple of pens, and my laptop and headed toward the dining table to begin my masterpiece. I started doing some research on my laptop. The first search was how to write a movie? I just want to say you can find anything you need on Google search. Little did I know Google search and I would become the best of friends. The first search results told me I needed to create a good script. Here I go again. Let's find out how to do that too.

I must warn you I have never written a script. It gave several sites that could help me, but this was definitely out of my comfort zone. As I was writing this script, I was learning a lot about myself and healing my depression at the same time. I created characters that were based on my life experiences of myself and the people I had encountered with. The next two weeks were emotional for me. I cried and laughed, which turned out to be a therapeutic experience. Life was going on for people around me. They paid no attention to what I was embarking on, but I knew I had to continue. It was like a divine spirit was guiding me to complete this task.

Now, I had an energy of purpose. See, this script was my first manuscript where I taught myself healing through words. I had a premise. I had an outline for the story. But I needed a storyline to connect it all together. I had to meditate and pray through it. I put a piece of me in the script. I laid out the characters with their own story. I had seen it done in many movies. I felt I could do that. I may not have had the book education of the work, but my education was visual. For years, I collected movies and would break down the entire plot as if I was the director. Little did I know it would come in handy one day.

I slept off and on for those two weeks, taking 15 to 30-minute naps throughout the day. I sometimes would burn the midnight oil. Once I finished, I sat back and gave glory to the Almighty. I had gone through this journey of healing by getting this script completed. I felt renewed and restored. I had never experienced that process. It was the feeling of giving birth to a child. It was powerful! I knew God was there to guide me during those moments. The words were just coming out of my brain. It is happening right now, as I've been writing this book. It was only he who protected me and shielded me from what was going on in the household. I could not understand why I was feeling the way I was feeling, but God knew that something was amiss and it would come to light the way he designed it.

The script went far; It went to places I never dreamed of. It has blessed me over and over. I got the chance to meet people from all over the world. I have been in rooms and talks with millionaires, billionaires, stay-at-home parents, lawyers, agents, actresses, actors, etc. I have had strangers come up to me and tell me they could relate to the characters in my story. It has opened doors for some people to level up in their careers. I won my first screenplay award. It has opened doors to more creativity for me. It filled movie theaters on all its opening days.

My life is still ever-changing. I can connect with people I never thought about connecting with. All because I did the Will of God. This just goes to show that by having obedience and trusting in the Almighty, the fruits and blessings will come. For that, I hope this part of my journey has inspired and provided guidance to whoever needs it right now. I am proof that there is power in your prayers and healing in words.

Chapter Eleven

Marriage Truth

Note: (I wrote all of this before my husband's passing) I told you the year 2015 was a rough year. I was in my wilderness season. God was preparing me to begin my new season of adding a new mindset. God was ready to put me to work after he got my attention. And boy, did he get my attention! It was December 15, 2015, when the spirit reached me again. It is said that the twilight hours are when spirits are at their busiest time. Why? Because as we sleep, our bodies are in an unconscious state, but our brain is active. I can remember waking up early that morning, needing to look at the cellphone bills. This was something I never did. I would just pay the bills and go on with life. I woke up and got on my laptop to look at my husband's cellphone bill. I was being guided. As I was looking, I noticed on the bill several numbers that were repeated on his usage. As I was looking at the bill, there were calls I was noticing on the current bill phone calls were taken mostly in the wee hours. See, my husband worked the graveyard shift. I started wondering why there was so much communication going on with these numbers. So, being the woman that I am, I called one number. Now what is about to happen changed me. This is a feeling that I do not wish anyone to go through. I dialed the first number, and a woman answered the line. She seemed annoyed that someone called her, but I knew she was not asleep because she had just gotten off the phone with my husband (thanks AT&T). So, I asked who was I talking to? I cannot remember her exact words, but I can remember mine, "Well, I know you are not asleep because you just got off the phone with my husband" (mic drop). She was quiet. I asked questions. She kept playing dumb, telling me to talk to my husband. I told her, "Don't worry about that, I will, but I am talking to you right now." We exchanged words, and I hung the phone up on her because I realized she was one of those dumb bitches (forgive my language). I was wasting my time and energy on someone who does not have any morals, nor does she have respect for marriages. So, I called my husband and when he answered, I asked him about these numbers. He did exactly what I expected him to do. First, he denied them and then got angry because I invaded his privacy. Let's be clear: when a spouse pays the bills, there is no privacy. I am just going to put that out there. Long story short, we separated that weekend.

Those last days were tough for me, as I felt my heart break into a million pieces. I give thanks to my mom and my children for getting me through it. But that was one of the worst weekends ever. I had time to sit back and really examine the whole situation, which then pissed me off. See, the spirit had been trying to get my attention for a long time that this person was not true to who they betrayed themselves to be. I take full accountability for ignoring the signs.

Let's get back to the story. After being separated from him for a couple of days, I was getting ready to start my healing journey. I did not want him. He showed me who he was. He did not differ from any other man I had been with. Then my phone got a text from him, telling me he was coming back home. I did not want him back. In my eyes, he was dirty. He was like a used car. But it was wisdom from my mom, who suggested that I have a forgiving heart. She is the reason I had to hear him out. I wanted to let sleeping dogs lie where he was. I say that to tell you now because we are still together. It took other married women and a lot of prayers to continue this journey. Why would I let someone else stake a claim in what I have built? True enough, their relationship did not end then, but my life was going in another direction. God was opening doors for me in other ways, and I could see my purpose was so much bigger than what I was living. By God's plan for me, my husband took notice. Things in our marriage changed. There were still issues of trust, but that was understandable. Some days were good, and some were not so good. But here he says, "We are stuck with each other." If I had a problem with him one day, he would be okay with that because he understood the role he played in all of this. He confessed to others how he hated that he ever did that. Because it was not worth the pain he caused. I never had another conversation with that woman because we were a different class of women. But if I ever had the chance to speak to her, it would go like this:

I am extremely grateful for your purchase of my book and wanted to take a moment to thank you. You've always been my number one fan. Yes, you are a fan. See, you follow my every move, whether it be physical or social. I do not hate you. Hell, I too would be impressed by myself. But I feel so sorry for you because you devalue your own self-worth and values that God has given to you just for pleasurable moments. I am convinced that this is true because of your repeated history of committing heinous adulterous acts with married men. You can't expect that this is pleasing on any level of spirituality. There are consequences to your actions, whether it be in this life or the next. It is not for me to judge you by how you choose to live your life. There is a plan for you too, I am sure of it. Although I did not give you the beating you were due, it is important to understand that my calm behavior and demeanor should not be viewed as a sign of weakness. That I am not! Why do you think God chose me to Grace your life? I will tell you. The attributes of being stronger, smarter, wiser, and forgiving are a reflection of the hardships I have faced and my ability to overcome them. I am here to teach you all those qualities. See, you already learned something; you are reading my book.

Now, back to business. You asked why I am still here? Obviously, this person has no respect for you or your marriage. See, let me break this shit down. One of the things I have learned about marriage is that it encompasses both a personal connection and a business partnership. Our shared belief is that our spiritual union can offer us certain advantages, and this is something we both agreed upon. The projection of it extends beyond the limits of our worldly perception, appearing much larger than what we see. Our purpose for being here is to gain a unique perspective on life and the journey we are on. I'll save this teaching for another day. God put me here. He sent me to be a blessing in his life and vice versa. God put us here in this life to help each other achieve our blessings and to be of service to him. I am anointed and blessed by God to help those who he has chosen on my journey. I am the blessing. I am loyal. I am faithful. I am one of many who God put to work to help his children. He had to learn from me, and I had to learn from him. So, when you hurt me, you hurt yourself.

We started this union out on hopes and dreams of growing old together like most couples do when they pledge their life together. This union was an investment way back then. People who know me know this to be true because they were there from the beginning. When we got together, he was in college and I worked a full-time job, raising four children, living on my own, and having my own things. I was paying for my lifestyle to support my children and myself.

So, when I opened my heart and home to someone, that person got full access to everything. They got access to my family, my children, my home, my vehicle, my finances, and my loyalty. I am an open book. What you get is me and no games and no mask. My mom and dad instilled in us kids to always be honest with people. It takes up too much time to chase lies after lies. Eventually, those lies will catch up to you. Then you must ask yourself, "Is the lie benefiting me? Does it have value in my life? Why do I have to lie?" If you have no answer to those questions, you might need to reevaluate your situation.

Getting back to the point I was making, I knew what he could become because he had goals and dreams just like me, and for that, I value him and respect him. I saw potential and wanted to build a life with him because he had goals and ambitions. I saw it in him, so I knew right then he was worth it. He had dreams just like I did. So, I worked while he found him. At first, he had no job where he got paid a paycheck, but he took a job that was equally important for both of us and that was helping with raising our children. This group of people is one of the greatest creations, our kids. No, he is not the father of them all, but that's a whole other story.

This was a full-time job within itself. This is one of those investments I was speaking about earlier. See, someone had to handle attending school meetings and after-school pickups. It goes both ways. That is another reason I did not walk away. Not to mention the hours spent helping him get his degrees, all of them. Yes, that was me from working, paying the bills, typing school papers, and contributing to tuition. Yes, that was me. Where were all these bitches who want to lay claim to something that I did? Sorry for the profanity. It took me out of character for a moment. But the thought of another who was trying to lay claim to what I built. Just hit a nerve. Were you that easy to entice? Don't even get me started on the sacrifices that were made. Only a small group of people know about those. See, few only talk about me being a stay-at-home wife. They only voice their opinion on what he did for me. But honey, let me tel you something. It went both ways. Don't act like you got amnesia and don't remember. Because I do and so do others. They say I should be for the materialistic things that were given to me. Hell, I earned, invested, and deserved every bit of them and then some. The tables could have easily been turned.

But that was a value and quality I learned from the women in my family and that was to honor godly commitments. To me, it just wasn't worth the risk and the headache. Now I could have been loose, like so many other women do when they are scorned. Believe me, the opportunity came more than once. I get hit on often. I will tell you this: some invitations have come from the people he knows. Another thing that kept me from choosing that good karmic path was my faith in God, my personal values, and the respect I have for myself. Besides, I am raising three boys and a girl and they need to see some type of positive role model.

As I stated earlier, my family background sets high standards for a person's character and morals. I was raised by strong women that work hard in every aspect of life without subjecting their body as a resource to get ahead in life. There I go again, getting off track. But you get the point. That is why I stayed. Yes, now and then I get in my moments. Sometimes, it's hard to heal when you are healing by yourself. Especially when you are living in the same environment that made you hurt. But what I learned about GOD is that he can get you through your dark moments. All you have to do is learn to let go of the past. Let go of the resentment. Stay the course. Don't give up, no matter how hard it is. If someone doesn't love you, love your-self! If someone doesn't respect you, respect your-self! Know your worth and your worth will know you! Don't let anyone take your self-confidence or your self-worth! You are here for a reason! God got you!

Chapter Twelve

Devil Within

Now I know God is still working with me and through me. Because baby, I have been going through it! It's like every time I am getting ahead, something jumps in and says, "What the Hell? Oh no, this is not what we are about to do here!" At first, I thought my eyes were playing tricks on me and my tortured mind was being tested. But one sometimes must accept that the truth is staring you right in your face. No matter how you try to sugarcoat or justify the way someone behaves or talks, it is the real them. We all have done this before. Asking God for some clarity or a sign to help guide us, yet most of us are unwilling to acknowledge the truth of clarity that God is showing us because we want it to work out in our favor. For myself, I once believed in treating others how they treat you. Meaning that if you are shady with me, I am going to be shady with you. This was my personal motto that I lived my life by.

I am wiser today because of the experiences and people that I have met on my journey. I now know people will treat you how you expect them to treat you if you are beneficial to their needs of you. Manipulative people have only one agenda, and that is taking care of themselves and themselves only. People do not sit back and evaluate their own actions before they act on it or speak about it. They are only concerned with how they feel and no one else's feelings. Today I also learned people do not know how to change their behavior. They have lived that way for so long and no one ever challenged or told them about themselves. People just learned to accept their ways and say, "Oh, that's just the way they are." Remember, I got some of the rebellion, I go against the grain, For that, I will not accept someone's behavior when I feel they are wrong or lying. That's just me. I can't do it and won't do it.

I cannot let a person think that everyone else's needs do not matter. Some people will only look after their own wants and needs. They will pretend to befriend people only to get what they can from a person. You can put them up in your house, pay all the bills, and they will still pretend to befriend you. The whole time they are using you and talking about you behind your back while you are taking care of them. Words today are just mere words. There is no honor, no integrity, and no loyalty. Now I am not in any way venting, I am just stating what I experienced firsthand with people who have agendas that are not aligned with the greater purpose. If you remember nothing from this book, please remember this: Do not eat everyone's fruit that is given to you. You cannot control what someone says to you, but you can control how you respond and converse with those individuals in your life.

Some people carry negativity with them. They are here to keep you from achieving what God has for you. It's not that they are bad people, it's just that their spirit has a weakness, that the devil can easily attract himself to their energy. They can easily be manipulated to do his bidding. In this season of my life, I've decided that anything that's not for my positive spiritual growth is not worth having in my life. Now there's so much more I can say in this chapter. I can really put certain people on blast who've done me wrong in my life. But this is not what this book is about. It's about spiritual growth. It's about taking in all the negativity and turning it around and not letting it consume so much of your life. It's not healthy to hold on to anger, jealousy, resentment, or how someone treated you. Let them go. Let it go. People have the right to add and delete whoever they want to from their life. Your question to yourself should be, why are you the deleted one? Remember, even books have endings.

Chapter Thirteen

Forgiveness

It had been a long time before I felt like me again. The last four years of my life were some of the best years of my life. My kids were grown and living on their own. We had several grandkids coming into our lives. Which means celebrations with the family were growing. My husband took a traveling job to get more money in our household. I was a stay-at-home wife. This was something my husband was satisfied with. He preferred it that way. I have to put that out here publicly because some who were not in our marriage seem to have a problem with that. Which I could not understand when there was only him and me on our marriage certificate. You know the part that said Mr. and Mrs.

He never made it a secret about me being a stay-at-home wife. Those who really knew him knew that to be true. He would say, "My wife doesn't have to work as long as she does these things: budget our home, cooking, keeping up appearances, and relations. I am a happy man." After all, I did it for him. There was a time when I worked, and he was a stay-at-home dad. That is what relationships and marriages are about. Working as a team for a greater purpose. We lived and believed in that until his last days.

I stayed busy doing something. I always had a side hustle. This allowed me to open the channels that God was preparing for me. I forgave my husband for his betrayal during our marriage. He and I had candid conversations that brought us back to what attracted us to each other way back then. He knew of this book I was writing. He encouraged me to get it done because he wanted to write his book. He would say, "Just don't talk about me too bad." He knew I would put that part of his betrayal in this book because it was a part of my story, my truth.

I put that part of my story in this book so those who are in relationships know that there will be times when there is no balance in the marriage. Sometimes things will be up and sometimes things will be down. Disagreements will happen. But just know and re-member you came together for a reason. Our marriage was predestined, to hear my husband say it. He used to tell me all the time about a high school trip he took one day to my high school. He had walked down the hall on that day when we were changing classes. He said he heard the spirit whisper in his ear, just as loud and clear, that the woman he would marry is in this hallway.

Before he departed his human form, I can truly say I learned a lot and did a lot with this man. The last years were just like our first years. We did everything together. Wherever he went, I was there. We ate together! We partied together! We got manicures and pedicures together every Friday. We woke up in the morning and planned our day out. During our entire marriage, we had only been a part for a few days. He made sure that we checked in on people that we were close to. Even if we stopped and visited for 15 minutes or a couple of days. Being on the road brought us closer and made us aware of what was important in life. He would say, "At this point in our marriage, we were stuck with each other." Neither one of us had the energy nor the patience to get back on the dating scene. We just wanted to grow old together and spoil our grandchildren. I can remember our last road trip. He was feeling a little under the weather with a sinus infection. He still had the zest for life, always wanting to go do something. On the way there, it was not an easy ride because he had some unsettling issues that caught him before we left. He just did his normal thing and put it all behind him and kept it moving because he said he wanted to make the most of his off days and time. We enjoyed ourselves that weekend. But the drive coming back home was different. We were listening to his playlist, and the energy was different. It was pleasant, and the senses were heightened.

I had time to sit back and really think about those moments. As I go back and revisit, I can remember us holding hands during the drive. We noticed our surroundings around us, such as the background scenery of God's land, as if it were a 3d painting. Everything was so crisp and clear. It felt like we were in heaven. Most of the time, we were the only vehicle on the road. We were just taking in the beauty of it and enjoying the feelings we had for each other. I must confess if that was a taste of heaven. I want more! It was pure love! It was serene! It was no worries! It was beautiful. I know for me that is where my husband is, and I will be ready to see him when God calls me home. I was glad that my last time with him was beautiful.

Chapter Fourteen

Keep it Moving

What the hell just happened? Did this woman just flip on me? I understand you may have felt overwhelmed, so I suggest you take a moment to catch your breath and collect your thoughts because what we are about to do is not what we stand for. There was a misconception that it was the case, but it actually wasn't. During the challenging period of losing my spouse, I gained the knowledge that snakes, regardless of their colors, forms, and statues, exist everywhere.

Over several years, I have faced the challenge of interacting with an individual who is very acrimonious. And now enough is enough. My bad for those who don't know what that means. It means bitter, angry, jealous, and negative. Give me a moment, let me come back. But you understand what I am saying. I can only explain this person this way, without offending my readers and sticking with my convictions of not bashing someone's identity.

But I will speak the truth about my experiences and how I choose to deal with the issues. I have never been the type of person who gravitates to gossip. I do not welcome it in my life, nor do I stand to hear it. So, when it's spoken in my presence, I try to change the subject or make the person who speaks on it find the good in that person. I try to change the narrative. My husband used to always say that's another reason he loves me because I always try to see the good in people. Which is true, I do. But don't get it twisted. When I see the ugly side of a person, I take action. I obliterate you from my energy. I pray on it. Because I know at that point, I have exhausted all my means of seeing how a person brings positivity into my life. I try to find good apples from their tree.

Here's an analogy I use and live by If I keep picking rotten apples from a tree and no good ones grow and the roots of the tree are dying, that means the soil is bad. Something deep-rooted and rotten within has spread throughout the healthy parts of the tree. All it takes is just one seed to find its way out to grow in good soil to be re-birthed into a glorious, healthy tree. That healthy tree can provide and give so much more to others in need. It has a purpose. But when it is damaged and nothing good can come from it, anything and everything within it will die. And guess what? There will be no signs of it ever existing. So, I ask you, how would you like your tree to grow? For me, I want my tree to provide purpose even after I am long gone. So, live your life with purpose.

Take a stand for yourself. Release the negativity and keep it moving. You don't have to put people in their place to make yourself feel good for a mere few minutes. You don't have to have the last word. Know that you have done nothing wrong. You do not owe anyone anything. I had to tell myself over and over that information. Because people were coming at me with their hands out, wanting a piece of what they thought was this massive inheritance after my husband's passing.

What I have learned about is the word "entitlement". Just because you are a mother, father, son, daughter, niece, nephew, aunt, uncle, or the damn dog does not give you entitlement to what a spouse has. Let me explain that theory and the law. Marriage is a contract between both parties and them alone. What they have accumulated together belongs to those in a marriage. If there is a will, it will stipulate the assignment of inheritance. But if there is no will, no succession, and the listed beneficiary is at 100 percent. The property belongs to them and them alone. If that person gives anyone anything of any size or any amount, it is done from them and from the heart. Don't expect that you are entitled because you played a position in that person's life.

My husband used to tell me, "Babe, I am telling you, they are coming. They're going to be the ones you wouldn't expect to cause you the most grief. I don't want that for you, but I know my people. So, I am telling you now, you don't owe none of them anything because I gave to them while I was here. That is your gift to do as you see fit. Take some to bury me and go live your life." I tell you what, the last few months have been hard mentally and emotionally. And he was right. The storm came, and I literally had to go through the storm alone. So, I did what he asked, and I gave some anyway to those whom I felt he would not have minded, but yet some were still not satisfied. They felt like they were entitled. I wanted to ask them, "Show me the receipts for what you have paid and contributed to this marriage! Show me the receipts when I carried the load when my husband was in school and I worked all the time! Show me the receipts when you came to my house and washed your clothes using my water and electricity! Show me the receipts when my vehicles were used as your taxi-cab when you did not have transportation! Show me the receipts from when you lived in my home, all bills paid! Show me the receipts when you got money for keeping our children when my husband and I wanted a date night!" See, I have all those receipts! I can go on, but I won't because there was no need. I hate to go there because that is not who I am. Because I give and expect nothing in return.

But when someone calls you and asks you for more and you already gave them what they asked for and then some and they tell you it wasn't enough on what you gave, that's where you have to draw a line. Or, how about a few hours after your husband's funeral, you tell them about the debt that you are about to face concerning their living whereabouts and husband's funeral cost, and that same person who told you what you gave to them was not enough says that is not their problem. Well, at that point, there is no love lost and none gained. The ride is over. This is where I leave you and let God handle the rest.

There are so many things that a person goes through when they lose a spouse. There are debts involved. Obligations that still have to be met that do not include anyone but you. In my situation, several people were looking at the financial gains of what they thought I was getting. But did not concern themselves about what I had to pay out of pocket before my husband's memorial and after his memorial and still to this day.

My husband and I had a plan in place when that time came for either of us. I did not need to prove a point or get anyone's permission. So, I say this, "Show me those receipts, when you speak of me not contributing the way you felt I should have or the lies you tell. As my words in my husband's obituary said, I will have a 'servant's heart, not a 'fool's heart.' Serving people comes in other forms of life. That includes words, endearment, compassion, food when someone is hungry, or clothes when someone needs clothing.

Speaking lies of me or my character, you rob people of a chance to know me, a child of God, that I AM! You have given them a false narrative of God's child, a false narrative of who I am as a person. All because of your inner hatred and jealously of me. For that, you will be judged, not me."

Because God knows it all! He knows what I did! He knows what we did as husband and wife! He knows what you did! I can truly say at this moment and the remaining days of my life; I gave love. I gave joy. I gave peace. I gave honesty. I gave a home. I gave what I could and I am very grateful to God for the blessings that he gave me to give with no expectations in return. Remember to give and expect nothing in return is acy of love from God. If you are counting everything you do for someone and you are expecting a return, know this: you are not giving with the love of God.

Chapter Fifteen

The Palindrome Day

It's been months since I heard your voice. 03-22-23 to be exact a Palindrome date. Since I felt your touch. Yet, I still push on. I used to hear people talk about a void in their life. It's like a part of you is just gone! Your mental thinking is not clear. I mean, you can still function and move around with your abilities. You just move slowly. Your reflexes are not as fast as they once were. That's how I have felt in the last few months. But somehow, I can still feel God and his angels around me. I can even sense my husband's spirit around me now. I could not at first. I guess during that time, life had taken hold of me. I was not open to receiving anything; I was too busy giving out. I was worried about everyone around me and made sure they were emotionally and physically okay and had the necessities of life. Not realizing that I would never see or touch this person ever again on this side of the realm. I was in the denial phase of it. I mean, I went through physical and emotional it because re-sponsibilities fell upon me. It was my job and duty to see it throughout. I had never ever been in a situation like this before. I mean, I had to deal with the death of a family member before, but never this close to my heart. I mean, this was my heart and part of my soul.

A part of me died on March 22, 2023. The part that was my overseer, my counselor, my pastor, my physician, my healer, my provider, my friend, my companion, my partner, my everything, and my me. I never knew the extent of it until a few weeks ago, after everything in my life paused and I saw it for the first-time playback in my mind. I often go back to that day at the hospital. I was there in the emergency operating room watching my husband lie naked before his coworkers fighting for his life. They were doing everything to save his life; I saw a line of healthcare workers taking turns to save him. When one would get exhausted doing compressions on his chest, another would step in. The doctor standing next to me was giving orders in her trembling voice but maintaining her composure as the commander-in-chief. Nurses were injecting syringes of medicine, hoping he gives a sign of something. At that moment, I realized, "Oh Shit! This is real! I am not dreaming my husband is literally fighting for his life." I grabbed my husband's phone and immediately called a close friend of his. I told him I need him to be strong and go do something for me. I explained what was going on. I needed him to go be with my husband's mother. I needed him to go to her and be with her. I would call him, or he would call me when he gets there. Then I called a friend of hers that I knew to go there. I told her what was going on. At that time, my husband's friend did not go. Instead, he did the opposite of what I asked him to do. He called my husband's mother and told her over the phone. My husband's cell phone started ringing. I answered the phone, not sure of how to tell her what was happening at that moment. Not knowing how she will take it. Is someone there by her to address any medical needs if needed? I am trying to remain calm to advise her of the situation, but before I can say anything; she was already there. Her emotions were so bad that the nurse grabbed the phone from me and explained to her what had happened. The doctor had asked me where the funeral home was located. I told her the location and name. I can hear my husband's mother saying on the speaker, don't call them. I had to stop her real quick and said that is who my husband told me to use. At that point, the nurse saw how this energy was going with her at that moment and that she was not helping the issue at hand. I cannot tell you what happened at the end of that call. Because I needed prayers. I needed spiritual help. I needed to pray, but I couldn't find the words. They are not coming out! Oh, Lord, help me, Jesus! What am I supposed to do? Why is my mind blank? What is happening to me at this moment? I cannot talk, I cannot move! I can hear voices around me saying, Ms. Yolanda! Ms. Yolanda! Are you okay? I hear one voice say, he's not coming back. The doctor gave another order of instructions to keep going. Deep down, I am praising her for her dedication and for going over and beyond her duties. I am thinking back to all the conversations we had and he would tell me how they put their heart and souls into saving a life. Never thought that I would witness it on him. Someone grabbed my hand, and I looked down and saw my cell phone in the other hand. I immediately called the one person who could help me pray. If you were to hear her pray, it's like she was right there in God's ear. I have seen how powerful and emotional her prayers are to God. My mom! She answered quickly; I said I need you to pray; I need you to pray like you never prayed before. I told her I was right beside my husband's bed, and I was watching my husband die right before my eyes! I need you! My mom got in her almighty powerful voice, and she prayed. The room started filling up. All kinds of workers came in and joined in the prayer. Some workers never stopped using their life-saving skills. I turned to look at the doctor as she and I made eye contact. It was a moment I felt that this was it. I knew what she was about to say. Until I heard this loud gasp of air come from my husband's direction. I turned my head and looked back at the doctor; I asked her, was that him? She looked at me and said, "Yes! That was him!" I looked back at him. This time, his head was turned in my direction and his glazed eyes were looking at me. At that moment, I was holding his hand. Wanting him to grip my hand tightly, like he does when we hold hands. I am talking to my husband, giving words to tell him to fight it and come back. His vitals are fading up and down, so I know he is fighting. But I knew if he came back, he would not be the same. See, they had been working on my husband for about an hour and a half. Having no oxygen to the brain for that long is never good. But I was willing to take that chance. I just knew I needed him here. But then the doctor gave her last instructions. "We will see if he does it on his own," she said. All hands stopped working. By that time, the room was full. I can see out of the corner of my eyes people are holding hands. I am staring into the soul of my husband's eyes. I can see his eyes filled with water and his heartbeat was slowing down. At that moment, I felt my heart racing, and I knew he was leaving. Everyone started leaving the room. I just sat there in the chair gazing at him, watching his vitals go down, and then hear these words from the doctor, "I am calling it." I was allowed some minutes alone with him to absorb what had just happened. And then someone said to me I need to call a mortician. They asked about donating his organs. I remember I could not talk about that. I just wanted to be left alone. Truth be told, I wanted him out of there. I wanted us both away from the hospital. I called the one mortician that my husband told me to call if something like what I experienced had ever happened. Then someone came again to me about donating my husband's organs. I remember saying loudly, "Give me a minute, I am still trying to process what just happened!" All I wanted to do at that moment was go back home, collect myself, and let out these emotions that I was going through at that moment. I just need to get there in a hurry and fast. For me, that was where everything about my husband was; at home, in our sanctuary.

Those are the moments that I was dealing with daily. Maybe my own prayers could have saved my husband? That was the constant battle I was dealing with since his death. I can finally say that I have accepted it. It was God's will. It was supposed to happen that way. That was the way my husband would have wanted it to be. Fast and no pain. He talked about death to me several times and always said that was the way he would want to go if he had the choice to choose. He got his wishes that day.

Healing is not something that comes quick and easily. It definitely takes time. But know you are not healing alone. It takes the love and support of a loving village. Sometimes we go through life looking at all the hardships we experience, whether it be death, financial woes, or health issues. We linger and hold on to the anger, the hurt, the disappointments, and the depression that we forget God is there to carry those burdens to build us up to reach his kingdom of heaven. More like a version, he has always seen in us, but we have been so distracted with the here and now that we forgot about the Alpha and the Omega. The beginning and the ending. There is joy after misery. There is healing after sorrow, there is happiness after hurt, and there is life after death.

Throughout this journey, I have shared with you my personal traumatic experiences, hoping that this will be a guide and an inspirational tool that helps you to understand you are not alone. All of us go through some things in life and it's okay to talk about it. This is how you heal. God showed me some years ago that writing was my healing. It doesn't matter how old or young you are; it is never too late or too early to start your spiritual journey. This life is just another stepping stone to what's next for you. Your journey is for you and you alone. No one will stand in front of your "BOOK OF LIFE" but you and God. He will show you your life; not your son, not your daughter, not your mother, not your father, not your spouse, not your neighbor, but YOU! You will be held accountable for what you gave and what you didn't give, and what you did and what you didn't do!

I know there will be naysayers out there wondering why I wrote this. If you must know, it was God's will. I was told by him years ago to do it. He gave me a gift of writing and told me to use this tool to share my words to help someone. If you know God, you already know how he follows through on his commands. He will definitely show you he means business. The longer you take to do his will, the longer you will wait to see what he has planned for you. Remember, he is a patient God but he is also a God of action.

Acknowledgements

Acknowledgements

My heartfelt appreciation goes out to all those who have supported me and provided me with the courage I need. I am incredibly grateful for your support and assistance, and I wanted to say thank you from the bottom of my heart. To those who lent me a listening ear during my difficult time, I extend my heartfelt thanks and appreciation. The ones who were there for me in my time of need, thank you. I want to express my gratitude to those who cried with me during my tough times, laughed with me during my happy moments, and prayed with me during my spiritual journey. Thank you all! I thank those who understood my journey and the ones who were part of my journey, good or bad. Thank you. Life is what it is, it depends on what you put into it. If you put good, you will get good, if you put bad, you will receive bad. In addition, I want to take this opportunity to thank the many brothers and sisters who reached out to me after my husband's transition. Their kindness and support meant the world to me. Through the tough times, it has been your prayers, thoughts, conversations, messages, and phone calls that have been the backbone support that has helped us persevere and push through. Thank you all for everything!

You are such an integral part of my life that I cannot fathom the thought of embarking on any journey without each one of you. (Mom, Dad, Crystal, and Pernell) Thank you!

Constance, Veronica, Gabby, and LaSonya, thank you for your light, guidance, protection, and friendship. Thank you!

Words cannot adequately express the depth of my love and appreciation for my kids and grandchildren, as it is beyond measure and cannot be fully captured even with an abundance of ink.

Yolanda C. Avery, a multi-talented American, has made a name for herself as a screenwriter, author, and business entrepreneur. She originates from Louisiana, where she was raised. Yolanda had a dual purpose in her writing: to motivate others through her creativity and to provide spiritual guidance. Her work involves advocating for the sharing of personal journeys, which has had a positive impact on her fans as well as being a source of support for her family and friends.

Prayers in time of Need

It may be challenging to find reasons to move forward in these times of trouble, confusion, and uncertainty. Life has its own way of chasing every individual with specific challenges and hurdles. These troubles could prove extra annoying and costly to over-happiness is mental depression. Sometimes all we need is a daily reminder of comforting words of hope and inspiration from the divine source.

Prayers for Spiritual Healing and Guidance!

A Prayer for Opportunities and Blessings

Dear God, I am grateful for the life you have given to me. Thank you for being merciful and loving in my life. Thank you very much for everything you do for me. I pray for your continued blessings in my life. Please open new doors of opportunities for me. I pray you will also restore any opportunities that I may have missed in the past. Please open my eyes so that I may see all opportunities open to me. Let your blessings abound in my life, Ob Lord.

Guide me and help me encounter the right people in my life. Teach me to bear your voice when you speak.

AMEN

A Prayer for Protection during Travels

Dear God, thank you for the lives of my family today.

Thank you for all you do for us. I pray for our travels today. Whenever we leave our home, we want you with us. Be it on foot, in a car, in a plane, or on water. Please be our protection during our movements. When we travel, please protect us from accidents, robberies, and car troubles. Take us to our destinations safely and bring us back home safely as well. Protect our families and friends from bad travel experiences. Keep them as a bird keeps her nest. Bless us and preserve our lives for your glory. AMEN

A Prayer for Protection of Marriage or Relationship

Dear Lord, I pray for my marriage today. Help us in dire and confusing times. Give us the strength to keep fighting against evil plans concerning our marriage (relationship). Protect us from evil, destructive seeds that will ruin our union. Help us fight our battles together. Help us not lose the connection and bond we have in this marriage (relationship). Give us the grace to seek you when we lack direction. Keep our marriage (relationship) safe from intrusions from outsiders. Help us solve our problems. You who give life, please give life to our marriage (relationship). Let our children see our togetherness and grow in the family's strength you have put together. Grant us a long healthy life to take

care of our family. Make our children a living, shining example of the love we share.
AMEN

A Prayer for Strength and Faith

God, I pray for strength and faith today. Help me know more of your word and face all adversities with the confidence of victory. Let me move mountains with my faith and command things to fall in line in my life.
Let me conquer all the evil in my life. Let my words cause healing and life. Let my faith build all the broken pieces in my life. Help me remain strong and not be moved by any adversities in Jesus' name.
AMEN

A Prayer for my Family

Heavenly Father, please bless our families with your love and protect us from harm. Give us grace to forgive, and strength to overcome the difficulties we face, and keep us together through the bard times of this world.
I pray you continue to bless everyone in my family.
Please let them remember you in times of need. It is through you that all good things come. I pray you bless them with good things

in life. Please order their steps so they can be at the right place at the right time. Protect them from any evil plans of the enemy and all terrible misfortunes. Allow them to grow closer to you and know that you are a just God.
AMEN

A Prayer for a Relationship with God

Heavenly Father, thank you for the blessings you have given upon me. Thank you for your protection and guidance. I pray that you, lord, will assist me in focusing my thoughts on you and remaining in you. Guide me in letting go of any distractions that may interfere with my connection with you. Teach me to love you and keep me.
attention to you.
Help me keep my mind open to your truth. Let it serve as a constant reminder always to put you first, no matter what. Help me study your word more thoroughly and to gain the wisdom and understanding necessary to apply it in my life. When things don't go as planned, please remind me that your plan for me is better than what I believe. As each day passes, please strengthen my faith in you!
AMEN

A Prayer for Emotional Healing

God, come to my aid today because my soul is troubled, and my heart is in pain. Embrace me in your loving arms and remind me I am loved and adored.

Help me overcome this challenging period in my life. I feel helpless and broken and, because of that, I cannot seem to function properly. I pray for your strength, Lord. Strengthen my mind, my heart, and my body. Grant my mind peace and calmness and fill my heart with joy and love. Bring a smile to my face once again. Thank you, Lord, for your grace and patience.

AMEN

A Prayer for Strength

God, today I pray that you be my salvation and refuge. The troubles of this world are making my life choices complicated. Some days, I am tired and weak from all the obstacles that are thrown at me.

I come to you today to ask you to please send down your holy Spirit to comfort me and restore my strength.

I cannot go on without you, Lord. I need you in my life. I need your strength; I need your power and your courage to move on in

life. Help me to always look up to you and not worry about my problems. Help me persevere and not give up on my journey. Give me the strength to keep fighting and give me the patience to endure whatever is thrown at me.
AMEN

A Prayer for God's Purpose for My Life

Dear God, I am glad that you made me. Thank you for your love and protection throughout my life. Thank you for the family I came from and all the influences I have received in my life. I pray to you today that you show me my purpose on this earth. Show me the path that I have been destined to take. Lead me to know what I have to contribute to your kingdom. Make me aware of the talents you have hidden in me and let me explore them. Let me know my use and objectives in my life.

I pray for guidance and direction. Let me not move with my own intentions and plans. I cannot succeed without your love and care.

Grant me your grace and your favor to make the right choices every time. I know there are ways that may seem right to me but will end in disaster. Help me avoid those ways. Teach me to hear and listen to your voice. Teach me to obey your voice and your word. Lead me to your light and take me away from the darkness. Be my shepherd and keep me safe for all time.

AMEN

www.ingramcontent.com/pod-product-compliance
Lightning Source LLC
Chambersburg PA
CBHW061002050726
47592CB00003B/1305